Watch It Grow

Watch a Banana Grow

by Kirsten Chang

Bullfrog Books

Ideas for Parents and Teachers

Bullfrog Books let children practice reading informational text at the earliest reading levels. Repetition, familiar words, and photo labels support early readers.

Before Reading

- Discuss the cover photo. What does it tell them?

- Look at the picture glossary together. Read and discuss the words.

Read the Book

- "Walk" through the book and look at the photos. Let the child ask questions. Point out the photo labels.

- Read the book to the child, or have him or her read independently.

After Reading

- Prompt the child to think more. Ask: Do you like to eat bananas? Can you explain how they grow?

Bullfrog Books are published by Jump!
5357 Penn Avenue South
Minneapolis, MN 55419
www.jumplibrary.com

Library of Congress Cataloging-in-Publication Data

Names: Chang, Kirsten, author.
Title: Watch a banana grow / by Kirsten Chang.
Description: Bullfrog books edition.
Minneapolis, MN: Jump!, Inc., [2019]
Series: Watch it grow | Audience: Age 5–8.
Audience: K to Grade 3. | Includes index.
Identifiers: LCCN 2018016790 (print)
LCCN 2018019038 (ebook)
ISBN 9781641282543 (ebook)
ISBN 9781641282529 (hardcover: alk. paper)
ISBN 9781641282536 (paperback)
Subjects: LCSH: Bananas—Juvenile literature.
Bananas—Life cycles—Juvenile literature.
Classification: LCC SB379.B2 (ebook) | LCC SB379.
B2 C43 2019 (print) | DDC 634/.772—dc23
LC record available at https://lccn.loc.gov/2018016790

Editor: Jenna Trnka
Designer: Michelle Sonnek

Photo Credits: sikarin supphatada/Shutterstock, cover; Apollofoto/Shutterstock, 1; Artem Kutsenko/Shutterstock, 3; Oksana Klymenko/Shutterstock, 4; parasolia/Shutterstock, 5; gopause/Shutterstock, 6–7; Photo by Naynon/Shutterstock, 8; Anton-Burakov/Shutterstock, 9, 23br; natthawut ngoensanthia/Shutterstock, 10–11, 22tr, 23tl; gan chaonan/Shutterstock, 12, 22tl; Chuanchai-KOB/Shutterstock, 13, 22mr; kongkieat suraka/Shutterstock, 14–15; Naypong/Shutterstock, 16–17, 22bl, 23tm; Elizabeth Fernandez/Shutterstock, 18–19, 22br, 23bm; hanapon1002/Shutterstock, 20–21; NOKDUE/Shutterstock, 23tr; 123313711/iStock, 23bl; Maks Narodenko/Shutterstock, 24.

Printed in the United States of America at Corporate Graphics in North Mankato, Minnesota.

Table of Contents

Yummy Fruit

Mae loves bananas.

Where do they come from?

Banana plants grow
where it is hot and humid.

banana
plant

They need
lots of rain.

soil

They need
rich soil.

bulb

A farmer plants a
bulb in the ground.

A tall plant grows from it.
The plant has big leaves.

banana

flower

It has one big flower.

Bananas grow with the flower.

They grow in bunches.
Each plant can make
150 bananas. Wow!

bunch

Time to harvest!

Bananas are picked
when they are green.

They are not ripe yet.

They become ripe
before they are sold.

Now they are yellow.

Yum! Eat up!

Life Cycle of a Banana

How does a banana grow?

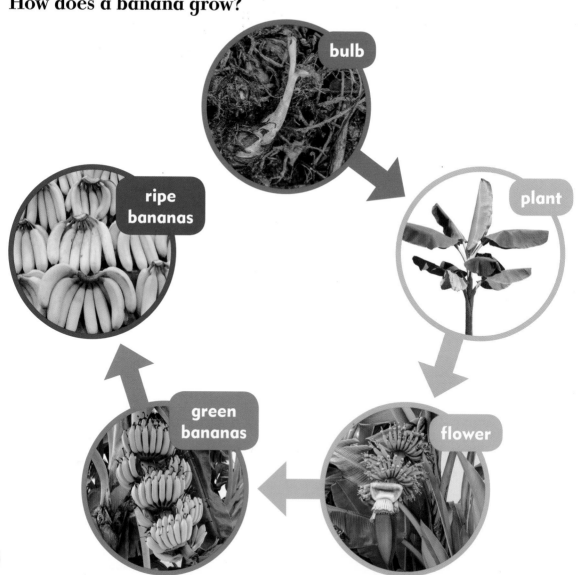

Picture Glossary

bulb
A round root that grows into a plant.

harvest
To gather crops.

humid
When there is a lot of water vapor in the air.

rich
Productive and fertile; rich soil is good for growing plants.

ripe
Fully grown and ready to eat.

soil
Another word for dirt.

Index

To Learn More

Learning more is as easy as 1, 2, 3.

1) Go to www.factsurfer.com

2) Enter "watchabananagrow" into the search box.

3) Click the "Surf" button to see a list of websites.

With factsurfer.com, finding more information is just a click away.